CHOOS

COMEBACK

PLAN

SUREFIRE METHODS TO HELP REINVENT YOUR
TEAM OR ORGANIZATION AFTER A CRISIS

ASHLEY PRISANT

First paperback edition June 2020

Printed in the United States of America

978-1-7351-5750-4

Squarepegsolutions.org

Table of Contents

Read this first!
How to use this book

The problem ... why you bought this book

In 2020, the world saw a crisis hit every business, town, organization, team, and group, not to mention every individual on a scale that no one predicted or imagined. Lives changed in every imaginable and unimaginable way. Organizations that had been doing business the same way for years could no longer sustain their business model. Employers sent staff home slowly, then at a more rapid pace, until nearly all employees were working from home (WFH).

How has WFH affected the organizations? How has it affected your organization? Perhaps WFH Employee productivity decreased over the last days and weeks – due to a variety of reasons – no one looking over their shoulder, the perception of not having to do so much, or maybe merely loneliness, boredom, or a lack of motivation (or all 3!).

There is an excellent chance that if your employee productivity was 100% in March 2020, productivity may have dropped 50 or 60% (or lower!) just two months later!

The purpose of this book is to help you address the following:

... How to think about employee productivity and engagement employees at the end of the crisis?

...What is the "New Normal"?

...How to manage the New Normal way of doing business?

... What is demand going to do?

...Relative to what it did the last few months?

...Do you change how business was conducted before the crisis?

... How do you prepare your teams to focus on what the organization needs from them – their best efforts to get past the crisis?

How to read this book

This book is a little different than most books you have read. In most books, you read page 1... then page 2... 3.. and so forth.

If you *Choose your Comeback Plan* in sequential order, you will get very confused, very quickly!

This book is about YOU. The book is written with YOU in mind. You will start on the first page and begin the story. You will read the bottom of the page, where you will receive   instruction on where to go next. You may be told to go to the next page, or you might be told to go to another section in the book.

Or... you could be given a choice. Do you pick choice #1? Go to that page. Otherwise, do you choose choice #2? Go to that (different!) page.

You will continue following your OWN story – until you reach the end of your story... or until you deviate and find another path. If you get to the end of the story, you have the choice to go back and try a different way.

Just like in real life for leaders of organizations, there are multiple paths, and no one way is "the best path." You have to pick the one that works best for you.

Additional Resources: You're not alone on this journey!

Just as in most organizations, you are not alone. The appendix in the back of the book is set up to help you along the way. You can use it on your journey, or you can read each Appendix independently. Also, the Reference section is constructed by areas (such as Strategy, Action Plan,

Motivation) to guide your direction to resources to help you develop your New Normal Action Plan. The goal is to help you to build your Comeback plan for your team, your department, or organization.

The bottom line-this story is about YOU.

This is YOUR comeback plan. What will YOU do next?

… turn to page 10 and find out.

Note on concepts & definitions

You may find the words Comeback Plan, and Pivot Plan used interchangeably in the story but there can be some differences.

A <u>Comeback Plan</u> is used to emerge from a situation – such as a crisis or a problem.

A <u>Pivot plan</u> is used to change the strategic course of a team or organization.

For teams or organizations that find themselves emerging from a crisis situation, bringing themselves "out of a hole" and needing something dramatically different – they will need both a Comeback Plan and Pivot Plan – so it will be the same.

Who should use this book

This book is meant to shake the tree a little… which means challenge the status quo. This book is especially designed for **small business owners**, **front line managers** and **mid-level managers** that are looking for ideas and inspiration on how to move forward after an event such as this.

You may be hit harder than most... you may be trying to survive. Or... your job may be ok for now, but you are struggling with your own motivation ... which makes it harder for you as a leader to LEAD.

Regardless of your position, this book will help give you ideas to move forward. Not all of them will work for you right now, in this position, at this moment. That's ok. Just promise me you will be open to the ideas that may work... that you may never have thought about... or thought couldn't possibly work for you.

This book is for you.

Let's get started.

Choose Your Comeback Plan

Congratulations. You made it.

All of the hard work you put in… meaning multiple conference calls, Zoom bombings, adjusting to new schedules, homeschooling, WFH (working from home), meetings in pajamas (at least the bottoms), and avoiding others … has paid off.

Your governor and other officials have released the stay at home order. Although it is slow and intermittent, the people from your company will be back to work in a week. Hooray?

But… why aren't you more excited? Why, although it's been more than X5 days, literally months since you've seen another person from work – are you feeling a knot in your stomach? Why do you feel apprehensive about going back to the place you've been going for a while – and seeing people that you knew?

Or thought you knew?

Perhaps it's because you don't feel you know what to expect. Maybe you don't think you know the job or the people as you did before. Perhaps they've changed, or maybe everything has stayed the same – and everyone at work entered a time warp from winter to summer. What happens to the goals and strategy the leadership so carefully laid out? Does it matter? Will there be (more) layoffs? Will things stay the same … and do you want them to stay the same?

You begin to think about what to do next. With only a week to go before everyone heads back to the office – or at least, the major part of the crisis in your organization is over - you don't feel like you have a lot of time. Essential questions – how are people going to handle our meetings after the crisis that hit our team like a bomb? Who will get laid of next? … are bouncing in your head.

And then the ACTUAL vital questions – what will my team want to do when I get back? What do I want to do? Should we change our strategy? Pivot our plan? – begin dancing at the fringes of your mind. Still – a lot is going on right now – and you're apprehensive that what was important to you before is not as important anymore.

You make a decision and start planning for next Monday. What did you decide?

- You choose to make no changes & do nothing out of the ordinary. You will start Monday – business as usual - Go to page 10
- You go on a trip & take a week-long vacation – Finally! You deserve it after these last few months. - Go to page 26
- You go back to work, but to be honest – you're not feeling it. It's not the same. That's what needs to be dealt with first. - Go to page 30

- You are feeling a bit uncomfortable with newness, change, and perhaps pivoting – but it's been uncommon ground for months. How can you push through – and maybe even help your organization and your team take advantage? Is that even possible? - Go to page 40

Seriously. It has been only a few months… or a bunch of weeks. What could change? Not much, not really. People talk a big game about change – but typically it's more talk than it's worth. They believe what is vital is staying the course – maintain what's going on – and being a strong leader for those stuck back there, always showing up and doing what they are supposed to be doing.

You get back to work… you walk into the office on Monday morning. Ahhh… there's almost a sense of homecoming. It's the same feeling you had when you returned from summer break, and you are starting the fall school term.. It's even complete with some of the stories. Tim from accounting shares one where his dog had puppies – and started growling fiercely during his 1x1 (one on one) with the big boss. Or Janice from R&D (Research & Development) whose family used up so much Wi-Fi bandwidth, they had to allocate hours of Wifi (but the hot water never ran out- probably because not everyone showered as much as they should have!)

You walk down the hall... say hi to your boss, John, in his doorway as you walk by (he barely grunts a hello as he looks at his computer) – wave to your team (you'll see them in about 30 minutes in the staff meeting) – and walk into your office. Ahhh. You close the office door. Time to start the day

- Go to page 11

There are many things to do. Before you know it, a week has gone by, and it's Monday once again. You are nearly caught on up the emails you ignored because they weren't necessary when you were WFH (work from home). Two projects landed on your lap last week – blah – and you feel like nothing ever happened, nothing ever changed.

You heard some senior directors talking about some changes they wanted to make based on all of the "post WFH" time – but you didn't pay any attention to it. It just feels like a time warp – and those guys just want to make a change for the sake of change. You don't want to be involved in that.

You head to your Monday morning staff meeting and realize something is going on. Laura and David, two more senior people on your team, are arguing – about nothing important (in your opinion). Holly seems to be preoccupied with her phone, and Roger looks agitated but trying to hide it by looking at his notes. Everyone else generally seems more lethargic and not into like they usually are. True... they never jump out of their seats, but at least they would do. .. something. Engage more.

What do you do?

- You want to dig more into what you could do to help them. - Go to page 12
- There's not much you can do at this point. It may just be your over-reactive imagination. It's Monday. It's happened before like this (right...?), and it will happen again. - Go to page 13

You don't know what you could do, but you can't do it by doing what you've already done. The results of what has happened thus far since you have returned has made it abundantly clear.

You are not comfortable with something new – but you are worried about the business surviving. You're concerned about your people leaving. Heck, you're afraid you'll have a place come back to in a few weeks.

- Go to page 40

You trudge back to your office. You meet with people when you have to. You do the tasks your boss tells you. You deal with events outside of your office, and your people come and go with questions. It's fine. By the end of the first month, you feel it's been like this forever – you almost forgot the previous crisis. Nearly six weeks later, it's like it never happened.

But something has happened.

The next week, your boss, John, calls you into his office. The numbers are down. "Well, obviously, John." You say, "Everyone's numbers are down. This crisis hit us hard."

He looks at you directly. "Not everyone's," he says. "Two of our five key competitors have seen an uptick in their numbers, and one has outperformed nearly every major metric we have – both on the financial and operational side. What are they doing post-crisis that we are not?"

He looks away, then looks at you again. "What is happening to your team? You've lost two people in the last three weeks."

You look up in surprise. Sure, Roger left, but it was personal reasons, right? Hmm .. it seems hard to remember. And… Amber left, but… well, that one was vague. You've been working – well, a lot of hours, right? A lot going on.

But… maybe you could see if something is connected. Is there something you could do? Is it too late? Let's be honest – trying to change things now would mean a colossal game of catchup. It's probably too late to change things. Isn't it?

- No, it is at least worth a try to see if we can change. - Go to page 14
- Honesty is the best policy, especially with yourself. Those points were anomalies... you think. - Go to page 15

You don't know what you could do, but you can't do it by doing what you've already done. This is abundantly clear. You've already lost ground, and the numbers are not looking good.

You've lost Roger and Amber. The reasons may or may not have been avoidable, but you do not want to test it out with another loss on your team. You read somewhere that every hire costs a company ½ to 2x a person's salary (McFeely & Wigert, 2019) at your level, and that's big bucks that you (and the organization) definitely could use somewhere else.

It's time to think outside of the box. You are not comfortable with something new – but you are worried about the business surviving. You're concerned about your people leaving. Heck, you are worried you'll have a place come back to in a few weeks.

- Go to page 40

It's an anomaly. An anomaly. It's now been almost two months since the crisis, and you have settled down. The business is .. ok. It is limping along. You realized that you had other priorities other than work, and you pursue them as well as carry out tasks for your boss. You challenge your team. You think things are going well.

They are not.

John, your boss, calls you into his office.

"Do you realize you could have just sat on your butt the last two months and got the same results?" He retorted. John was not usually an angry guy. He was one that had a lot of words to say, as a true extrovert, and sometimes you had to separate the good from what was necessary- but you didn't have to read between the lines. He was mad at you.

"No results. No impact. You didn't even try. I thought before all this started that you had potential. Now, it seems you're ok just going along with the status quo. Is that the case? If so, let me know, and we can have a different conversation. I can only spare so much time, and I need to get things done – but it will require more work. I need to see the impact in the next two weeks. I'm ok if you don't want to move forward – but you need to let me know that. Can you take the extra time and fix this?"

What do you say?

- "Two weeks, boss. You won't be sorry". - Go to page 16
- "I'm sorry, John. I want to be honest with you. I can't take on more work. I need to stay where I am, for now. I will help as much as I can" - Go to page 21

You don't know what he said, but he said it right. You now have a fire under you – to do something. You head back to your office with a purpose.

But,what are your next steps ? You look around your office and stare at the wall for a few minutes.

You start looking at your bookshelf. Yes, you seem to have the important topics – on management, leadership, organizations, etc. Blah. None of those will help you with a turnaround. We are managing through a crisis. Dealing with being at the top, then hitting bottom (or close to it).

You flip on your laptop and start Googling "Comeback Pivot Plan" and things like that. You discover something called the "5-3P" – Epilogue – 5-Piece Pivot Plan (5-3P) Overview. This plan was used by those organizations that turned around during a significant event, a crisis, or needed to pivot strongly – to grow, or just survive.

The plan looks like a 5-piece circle for the board game Trivial Pursuit, where you tried to secure as many of the pieces to "succeed" in the plan. (see Epilogue – 5-Piece Pivot Plan (5-3P) Overview) There were five areas:

1. Strategy rebound review
2. People pivot performance
3. Organization/ Individual – Gap comparison
4. Action Plan - Level the field
5. Carry out & Accountability - The final piece

It was an interesting concept – and you looked further at how it could be tailored to you… your team... maybe even a few ideas for the organization. Perhaps you should have thought about this months ago. Well. Can't cry over spilled milk now.

Go to the next page.

However, could you do it all in two weeks? Probably not. You read about the different areas – and started to plan what was most important. But what was "important"? What was suitable for the organization? Something to impress John? Was your job on the line? What areas should you go in to make the best (right?) impact?

- It could be worth a shot to look at strategy … even if you may not be entirely comfortable with it - Go to page 18
- It is about people. That is the organization's most important asset. You have to focus on that first. - Go to page 20

You decide to focus on the organization – the structure of the business and how to pivot. If you don't have money, cash flow, goods, services to sell – then even the most exceptional people could not help. You feel if you get the strategic changes, the foundation in place, the rest – although it won't be easy – will follow. You look at the Strategy People Worksheet (Appendix A - #1 - Strategy) and get going.

With a mindset of getting the majority of "the important stuff" completed, you work through the checklist and put together as much information you can. You question the current strategy; you look at where you are on the high/ low charts (are you starting from a high op tempo and are now at a low point – trying to ramp up? Where are the changes? The problems?

You present your results to John and a few other key managers. They are interested in the results, and Johns asks you about how it will improve the organization.

You explain the necessity of the "Pivot" – which is an opportunity to pivot your organization ahead of others in your industry as the industry and the country itself moves forward on strange ground. You want to take advantage of the timing by being aggressive with thinking what's next.

He asks some questions and gives push back on areas that you need to develop further. The CFO, Greg, appears to be having second thoughts, although he initially bought into the idea.

"I don't know… I think this is good… but it's too late to do much of this. Why don't you continue to do what you can for your own department and get back to us in a few months?"

Go to the next page.

Although you are somewhat disappointed, you realize you may only have yourself to blame. You had a hunch there was an opportunity at the beginning – but you were a bit hesitant to go out of your comfort zone – or rock the boat at the organization.

You continue on the 5-3P – 5 Piece Pivot Plan for your department. You are determined to do two things now.

1. Make the department a shining example of what the Pivot Plan could do for a group.
2. … and not be afraid to take a chance on something you believe is an opportunity for your team & organization at work.

<End>

You decide to focus on the people's side first. You dig into the People elements first. You feel if you get the people taken care of, the rest will be fine and fall into place. You look at the People Worksheet (Appendix B - #2 People Checklist) and get going.

With a mindset of getting the majority of "the important stuff" completed, you work through the checklist and put together as much information you can. You do interviews with your team and get the managers of other teams to do them, send surveys, or emails – as much as you can. You end up getting decent data… or at least it appears. Nothing looks out of place… nothing seems out of the ordinary.

You share your thoughts with other managers, and they start asking questions about their teams. You find out they learned a significant amount from talking to their people about the issues you asked them. They were shocked to find out <u>how many</u> people were affected, and more importantly,_how_<u>they were affected</u>. Some people acted like nothing at all had happened – but really, their worlds had imploded for various reasons. Others frequently were deemed "melodramatic," became calm and resolute in their post-crisis views. They were ready to help, and actually, a few ideas were recommended to your team.

You present your results to John. He's interested in the results, and he asks you about how it will improve the organization. You struggle to answer. You stumble over the concepts of the people … engagement…

"Ok.. people are important … and that is great and all.. but if we have no cash flow – no improvement in the metrics, then we can't do all these great things. You may be a good leader, but you have a lot to learn about managing a department."

Honesty is the best policy, right?

Your comment to your boss just minutes ago, "I'm sorry, John. I want to be honest with you. I can't take on more work. I need to stay where I am, for now. I will help as much as I can," rings in your head. You know it to be true, you know it to be accurate, and you know it wasn't the right thing to say.

What made you say it?

Something. You're not sure. It was about this crisis. It was about the months during … and the months before that. It was like the time a friend of yours died at 25, very suddenly. You were working long hours, getting pummeled by work every day, despite the long hours, and nothing added up. Suddenly, with his death – everything did. Why work this hard? Why drive yourself into the unknown – you don't even know you want?

You begin weighing your options. You realize you have several.

You talked to, Janice, from R&D (research & development) – who mentioned going back to school to get her Engineering Masters or her MBA (or even both!). She wants to make a career change. It had nothing to do with the organization, but it was more about finding something that was more *her*. Give her reasons other than a paycheck to get up in the morning.

You could... just let the inevitable happen. You can see the writing on the wall. John was NOT impressed with your performance and did not expect much from you. You also know yourself and know that you do not have the desire to "dance his dance" just to look good for him. If you get fired, especially during this time frame, while you're giving the "effort," then at least you can collect unemployment... which will buy you some time to figure out your next moves...

Go to the next page.

You could bite the bullet... and quit. It's fast, effective, and, more importantly – you have the control. You can say when, where, and how. You can play the game for a few weeks, line up a few things on the outside – and then make the jump. It can be your move.

Or... you could take a week to decide. Figure out what else you want to do – whatever that is. You could take a week off. Go somewhere that no one else around here is... and just go. Let your hair down and reconsider what your next move is.

What do you do?

- You remember the last recession and realize now is the best time to go back to school. - Go to page 23
- There really is no use waiting. Allow yourself to get fired - and move on with your life. - Go to page 24
- You'd rather be in charge. Time to quit and figure out who you really are -and what you really want to do. - Go to page 25
- You are not 100% sure... so instead of making a rash decision – try to figure out if you want to do something else. Take a trip to decide. - Go to page 26

You consider the options and surf the net some more. There are some pluses and minuses about going back to school. You could delay what will be happening to your organization (and pretty much anyone else's) by going to school. You could go into that area you've been interested in but never had a reason to leave. You would go into debt… but you're bored with your current life. Shouldn't you invest in that? In what YOU want to do?

In the end… you decide to go for it. You work out the next three months and give your notice. You start your new program and begin your 2-year program. The organization moves on; they have a small farewell for you. Before you left, your boss, John, wishes you luck. "I'll always wonder," he said, "what could have happened if you'd put your mind to making a change here in the organization."

Maybe you did too. But there's always time for that later—next time.

\<End\>

It's a done deal. You remember the flight attendant that grabbed some beers and jumped out the airplane chute... what a way to go! As much as you'd love to say "take this job and…" you're not that upset with the job... just with what it's doing to you, the people, the organization… well. Ok, yeah. It does kind of tick you off a bit —A LOT.

So. You sit back. And watch. You somewhat do the work. You feel a little guilty about doing nothing for your team – but your team does not seem to care, and neither do you. Yeah – maybe this is the way to go.

You get the PIP (Performance improvement plan) from your boss and promise to work on it. (yeah right). You continue down the path, waiting for the days that you just can sit back... and... well, who knows. Then you get the numbers for the quarter – they are not good. They will have to cut the workforce back 15%. Yes! This is your chance.

…and it is. The next day, John calls you into his office. You try not to look gleeful. He explains the situation … and they had to make some cuts. You put on a poker, almost sad, face, and accept your fate. He tells you to work out the details with HR for unemployment... and that's that.

You walk away from the organization with no regrets. At least initially.

A month or so later, you're sitting on your couch after your last binge-watching of your 10th new show. What would it have been like to try something new? To try this Comeback Plan – this pivot everyone is talking about? What would it have looked like if you had been a part of it?

Maybe there's a chance to try again.

Not one day more.

There's no reason to stay in a place that you don't want to be – and don't have to be. It's just a job. You feel negative all the time. This crisis made you focus on what's important. What are money and status if you don't have friends and happiness.

"John, I appreciate what you've done for me these last few years," you start the next day. "This has nothing to do with you – for the most part." You feel honesty is the best policy, right?

You continue, "I've been working on prioritizing my goals, and with what's happened the last few months. I'm giving you my two weeks. I'll be happy to help in any way I can, but will be moving on after that."

He looks surprised. "Where will you go?"

You shrug. "Honestly, I don't know. I'm looking forward to finding out."

You take a trip. It's been a while since you've been on a plane or in a hotel. Heck, it's been a while since you've even crossed the state line. You line up all the details (everything is still relatively inexpensive), pack a suitcase (almost forgot where it was) – and you head out.

Your boss is a little upset with you for leaving. Still, he understands – especially when you promise to take your laptop (okay, maybe where you're going doesn't have Wi-Fi) – and you'll work double-time with extra enthusiasm (in theory, right?).

You get to your vacation spot – a place, out of the way, with the basics of home (somewhat) with little issues. You sit back, relax, and enjoy something that is not your home office (also your dining room table). You have different foods and talk to the locals.

With two days left in your vacation, you feel refreshed. You've had a great time. You realize – you could stay here forever. You could probably get work here, or even start that small business in town you've always wanted. Hmmm.

- Maybe you'll stay… at least a while longer. - Go to page 27
- It's time to face the music. Those decisions won't make themselves. - Go to page 28

This is the life. Really. You remember hearing the phrase, "Sometimes you have to leap, and the net will appear" by John Burroughs. Why not just… stay?

Sure… you make good money back home – but what's there? The job you had would be a nightmare to try to fix, to solve – and to help try to solve all of those problems that were going on with those projects? Ridiculous. The most important thing is to try to fix *you*… and this may be what you needed.

You don't have to stay here forever… just. For now.

You give your boss, John, a call. You explain to him that you're giving your two weeks. "Wait a minute. I thought you were on vacation?" He sounds shocked.

You said… "Yes, I am… and for now, I'm going to stay here." You give him more of the details-and you will fulfill your two weeks. You initially offer to send all of the work material back at the end, but after a few more conversations – he suggests you holding on to the material. "Just in case." He may even have a project for you, later… which could do well if the local restaurants or retail stores don't need an extra hand. You may need that money. You agree.

Although you're not quite sure what will happen next, you've decided you're going to do your own pivot. The crisis made you see… when life gives you lemons, make lemonade.

For you, your lemonade is working in a place you love.

One week turns into two… and then one month turns into three months. You may go back; you may not. On your 100th night, you toast to yourself on your balcony. "Here's to the people who change… for themselves"

You realize that while it was a great vacation – it was just that. A vacation. A place to charge. A place to get your thoughts together and your head back on straight. Sure... it would be nice to stay here a while (or forever). But you don't think like that.

You know that you are needed back home. You *want* to be back at your job. You know that you have the skills necessary to help the organization. Well... maybe not everything needed to be fixed. You're not a superhero – but you know that you'd feel a little FOMO (Fear of missing out) if you stayed here. What was going on – and what could you have done/ contributed?

You head back to your home. The fewer the miles between you and work, the more the excitement wears away and the dread pools in your stomach.

You begin to think about what to do next. Everyone has already been back to work a week so.... You don't really feel like you have a lot of time. Important questions – what am I going to eat? What am I going to wear? How long will it take to travel – now that real cars are on the road? – reverberate through your mind.

And then the ACTUAL essential questions – what will my team want to do when I get back? What do I want to do? Should we change our strategy? Pivot our plan? – begin dancing at the fringes of your mind. Still – there's a lot going on <u>right now</u> – and you're apprehensive that what was important to you before is not as important anymore.

Go to the next page.

You make a decision and start planning for Monday. What did you decide?

- You make no changes & do nothing out of the ordinary. You start Monday – business as usual - Go to page 10
- You go back to work, but to be honest – you're not feeling it. It's not the same. Maybe that is what should be dealt with first. - Go to page 30
- You are feeling a bit uncomfortable with newness, change, and perhaps pivoting – but it's been uncommon ground for months. How can you push through – and maybe even help your organization and your team take advantage? Is that even possible? - Go to page 40

The week rolls on. You do some work. Bleh. You attend some calls. Bleh. Some people seem eager to go back... but to what? You were able to get it done at home. (Sort of) Nothing fell off the planet. (Sales did drop by 30%, but that's easy to recover. The organization has been around for a while. Besides that's not *really* your job...)

You're back to work on Monday. You pass your boss, John's office, and wave – giving him a fake smile you need to give him. *Fake it 'til you make it.* Especially with him. He's energetic. Exuberant. You don't have time for that.

What do you have time for? Work... It's not the same. To be honest with yourself – you don't respect the job, your boss or your organization quite the way you did before. You just... don't feel it. Too much and nothing has happened.

Still – you know you have to keep working. You're not depressed (you don't think...). It's just a rut. You flip on your laptop and get to work.

Go to the next page.

Days roll by. You feel better; you feel worse. You start talking to the members of your team (Really, out of boredom. You don't want to be working on the projects you had before you left. You had them covered when you were elsewhere, and now it's like you're starting over. Such a waste!)

You talk to Holly, who has two kids in elementary school. She had to homeschool them both and was excited just to be out of the house – and talking to grown-ups.

Or Roger... who shared a tiny apartment with his live-in girlfriend. He was glad to be in a room where she wasn't. Working and living with someone was a lot to handle. (So far, they were still together... at least for now).

You just can't share their enthusiasm. The projects don't work. The organization doesn't know what it's doing. John is too cheery.

What do you do?

- You figure it out. You find a way to get motivated - Go to page 32
- You need to be honest with yourself. It can't be done.. not right now. - Go to page 15

Ok. You've got to snap out of this. You don't feel it, but you know it won't be like this forever. You've been through worse. You take 5 minutes and think about your <u>crucible</u> moments. This is not the worse thing that happened. You're just feeling... slow. Maybe a little lazy. (Hmmm.. maybe literally. When's the last time you've set your alarm clock?)

So... you take a look at Appendix F- Motivation 101 for methods, and you select your approach. It is not easy. By the time week 2, then week three rolls around... you're doing... a little better. Nothing is moving the needle – either your team or you – but you're not surprised. You're getting through it. You're slowly changing your attitude.

At the beginning of week 3, John, your boss, calls you into his office. He's energetic, which is his personality, but the message is direct.

"I know you've been through a lot. We all have. It seems you're struggling... " All of a sudden, you feel angry – and a little embarrassed – at the same time. Why is he asking now? Why does he have to get into your business? Does he even understand?

... and maybe he does. Perhaps he's had his problems, but he figured out a way to self- motivate – or at least make an attempt. You struggle to maintain a poker face – or at least not look upset.

"... but right now, *we* as an organization are struggling. Cash flow is way down. Hiring is out. We have projects that may disappear if we don't do something fast. I may have to let people go..."

Go to the next page.

He continues. You realize where this could go. Well - you've been having problems yourself, right? The organization was here before you got there... and you weren't going to be there forever, right? Still – you are motivated by doing good work, and sometimes getting out of a sticky situation could be as motivating as the next project. But... that could be more work than you have the mental capacity to deal with right now.

He finishes his monologue and looks directly at you. What do you say? Can you handle more work?

- To be honest, you are more checked out than you realized. You need to focus on you - Go to page 34
- "Give me an opportunity. I'm not quite sure what, but I'll look into it." - Go to page 37

You realize…. It's great to be wanted. But what if you don't have the capacity to do the things that are requested by your supervisor… If you are mentally taxed and have just *hit a wall* … then, maybe you need to take a break. Not from work altogether, not from the job… only from… the push. From the constant pursuit and the always uncomfortable feeling of being pushed into areas, you don't know the outcome.

You go for a while. A week goes by. You work on the projects given; you provide some comments in meetings. You talk to your people, you're going through the motions, but life is starting to come back to you. You are beginning to see the bigger picture and realize you may be able to make an impact. You watched a fair amount of media while doing other things (all work was done when it was supposed to… of course!). You remembered several articles, podcasts, shows… of various people talking about how to help organizations recover.

One management consultant mentioned the reason her company stayed in business. "Leaders are great in many ways," she started, "but continuously, without fail, the two areas that trips leaders of all experience levels continue to be *communication* and *accountability*. Leaders don't talk the same language as their followers. Once they finally get their message across, they have an even *harder* time holding them accountable to whatever they asked for in the first place.

Another talked about getting the people on track. "I have three rules of leadership," she said. "Take care of your people, take care of your job, and never stop learning. If you make sure your people are covered – take care of their needs, understand where they are, where their heads are coming out of this – and challenge them to use their strengths – they will pull you out of this".

Go to the next page.

Still, another said, "Take it one day at a time.". He continued – "We do NOT know what's going to happen. To make big moves, big decisions, right out of the gate, could be a career if not organizational suicide. Take steps, evaluate what happens, and go from there".

You are ready to move on... you know you can't stay here. But with that advice ringing in your ear... what do you do now?

- You decide to take it one day at a time. Make sure to TRULY understand the impact before making a big decision. You don't want to make it worse for the organization or especially your team – they've been through so much. - Go to page 13
- You've got to follow through with what you started and hold people accountable to make this happen. - Go to page 36
- Something's different, but you're not sure what. You need to focus on what's changed for the employees to get to the bottom of this. - Go to page 46

Your team seems to know what they are doing (collectively), and the go-forward plan seems sound – so why bog them (and you) in all the details? Why go through all these steps that you really can't implement – not from your level at work (or your energy level right now – overall)?

So, you decide to follow the current strategy set forth by your company. You use Appendix A - #1 - Strategy to make sure you understand the strategy. You bring your team together… explain how they will do what they will do. The current strategy is only moderately changed from a previous one, so there are no big surprises. You get feedback. Not everything you thought of, but you're mostly there.

You use Appendix E - #5 Accountability Checklist Information to help guide your plan for holding them accountable. It works… the team moves in the right direction; your department gets better. The numbers move to the right… slowly. Weeks go by… weeks turn into months. You later realize you missed the big opportunity to make an impact. You hear about someone else doing it and wonder. Perhaps there will be a next time.

You feel something that feels like... motivation... surging through you. You feel a challenge coming on, and one you want to step up to.

You say honestly, " I'm not quite sure what this looks like, but I'll look into it. Give me a week, and I'll get back to you".

You remember a friend that may be able to help and give her a call. She answers on the third ring. Stephanie is in leadership in operations for a company that is known to be innovational in its management strategies. The company is in a different industry, so the two of you are comfortable sharing best practices regularly. She's also been a project manager before, has had over 15 years of leadership experience and has managed a variety of times in tough situations.

After the typical small talk and five minutes of catching up, you launch into your scenario.

"Stephanie... how are you guys doing over there? I have been looking at our numbers – like many, we struggled through the outbreak and had to let people go. I know you had to as well. How are you and your department managing 'after' this? I feel so many people focused on managing through it – that no one looked at what's after".

Stephanie laughed grimly on the phone. "You're right. I think most people, even our company included, were focused on survival mode. I certainly was at many points. However, I realized a few weeks ago that there would be an 'after' to all of this, and started doing some work, researching some best practices of my own, and have been working through those now."

Go to page 38

Eagerly, you ask her for more information. She explains that she called it theEpilogue – 5-Piece Pivot Plan (5-3P) Overview (5PPP or "5-3P"). She put it together after researching other "comeback" plans and ways that organizations have turned around during a major event, a crisis, or a need to pivot strongly. Her favorite game was Trivial Pursuit, so she imagined a 5-piece circle that needed all five areas to "succeed" in the plan. She lists five areas:

- Strategy rebound review
- People pivot performance
- Organization/ Individual – Gap comparison
- Action Plan - Level the field
- Carry out & Accountability - The final piece

She heard the hesitation in your voice when she asks if it makes sense. You feel overwhelmed. "This seems like a lot of work," you admit honestly. Your head is spinning. You don't have time for this. And if so, you may or may not be able to convince the others in the organization to go along with it. (see Epilogue – 5-Piece Pivot Plan (5-3P) Overview for more information on 5-Piece Pivot Plan).

She said, "Yes, and no. Some of these you may already know the answers to – and others may be areas you should have looked at long ago. This situation we've all been put in is unique. You have the opportunity to take advantage of it. Or Not. Maybe it's not right. What if it is?"

Go to the next page.

You talk for a few more minutes and then hang up. You sit at your desk, looking blindly at your laptop screen. It was a lot to take in. You turn it over in your head for a few more minutes. Something like this has never been done in your organization. Regardless of what she said, it would take work. And – there were convincing people to go along. To help provide information.

- The people are what make up this organization. They are the backbone, and you have to start there. - Go to page 46
- It's time, to be honest. This is too much work for now - Need to focus on you. - Go to page 34
- Yes! All of it! I don't care what it takes! - Go to page 43

You've decided to push the envelope, and try something new… but what does that mean? You talk to a friend, Stephanie, who is in leadership in operations for a company that is known to be innovational in its management strategies. The company is in a different industry, so the two of you are comfortable sharing best practices on a regular basis. She's also been a project manager before, has had over 15 years of leadership experience and has managed a variety of times in tough situations.

After the typical small talk and five minutes of catching up, you launch into your scenario.

"Stephanie… how are you guys doing over there? I have been looking at our numbers – like many, we struggled through the outbreak and had to let people go. I know you had to as well. How are you and your department managing 'after' this? I feel so many people focused on managing <u>through</u> it – that no one looked at what's after".

Stephanie laughed grimly on the phone. "You're right. I think most people, even our company included, were focused on survival mode. I certainly was at many points. However, I realized a few weeks ago that there would be an 'after' to all of this, and started doing some work, researching some best practices of my own, and have been working through those now."

Go to page 41

Eagerly, you ask her for more information. She explains that she called it the *5-Piece Pivot Plan (5-3P) Overview* (See Epilogue). She put it together after researching other "comeback" plans and ways that organizations have turned around during a major event, a crisis, or a need to pivot strongly. Her favorite game was Trivial Pursuit, so she imagined a 5-piece circle that needed all five areas to "succeed" in the plan. She lists five areas:

1. Strategy rebound review
2. People pivot performance
3. Organization/ Individual – Gap comparison
4. Action Plan - Level the field
5. Carry out & Accountability - The final piece

She heard the hesitation in your voice when she asks if it makes sense. You feel overwhelmed. "This seems like a lot of work," you admit honestly. Your head is spinning. You don't have time for this. And if so, you may or may not be able to convince the others in the organization to go along with it.

She said, "Yes, and no. Some of these you may already know the answers to – and others may be areas you should have looked at long ago. This situation we've all been put in is unique. You have the opportunity to take advantage of it. Or Not. Maybe it's not right. What if it is?"

You talk for a few more minutes and then hang up. You sit at your desk, looking blindly at your laptop screen. It was a lot to take in. You turn it over in your head for a few more minutes. Something like this has never been done in your organization. Regardless of what she said, it would take work. And convincing people to go along. To help provide information.

Go to the next page.

What do you do?

- It may be a long road, but the right thing to do is start with Strategy - Go to page 43
- It's time to focus on what still exists. There's a lot to do now. Better to focus a lot "closer to home" - Go to page 13

You grab a drink from the refrigerator down the hall and sit down at your desk. You've decided to pursue the Pivot Plan. You begin reviewing a checklist of items that you want to think about for the strategic piece of your plan (#1 – Strategy - on the 5-piece pivot plan) and begin working down the list.

First, you take a look at the resources, time, and elements that you need to do this. At a high level, – the steps are:

- Appendix A - #1 - Strategy– What is important to the organization? (Really important... now? Not just because it was important months ago). What has changed?
- #2 People – Who are they... now? What do they represent – to themselves and the company? How did the incidents from the last few months affect them?
- #3 – Organization/ Individual – comparison – What aligns? What may be in conflict? Which elements are most important?
- #4 – Action plan – There's the first iteration before you start (what you're doing now) – but what does it look like now that you have the info? What are the critical priorities? What is not so important?
- #5 – Accountability - How to make it stick? How do you get long term buy in to complete the pivot?

You start writing furiously.

Go to page 44

After hours, you emerge. You feel triumphant, and after a good night's rest, you present your data to the individuals in your organization that need to buy-in before you move forward.

You explain the necessity of the "Pivot" – which is an opportunity to pivot your organization ahead of others in your industry as the organization, industry, and the country itself moves forward on, strange ground. You want to take advantage of the timing by being aggressive with thinking what's next.

They ask some questions and give push back on areas that you need to develop further. The CFO, Greg, although he initially bought into it, appears to be having second thoughts.

"I don't know… I think this is good… but the full five steps will take too much time. I like what you've talked about here at the end – the #4 Action Plan. Since you've pretty much already addressed the other pieces in your recommended Strategic plan – can we just jump there? We're trying to pivot – so let's do it. Let's not waste time. We've got cash flows to worry about. I give it a few weeks, a month at max, to make an impact."

Your boss, John, chimes in and supports your cause. "Yes – I agree – but it's not as much time as you think. We need to do this thoroughly – and right- to get the max bang for our buck. This could be game-changing."

Greg stacks his papers and begins to leave the room. For him, the meeting is pretty much over. "I hear you, John. But I have shareholders to report to and a lot of inventory that won't sell itself. I still think we should go for a quick impact now. We can always revisit later, right?"

Go to the next page.

The meeting over, you look at your boss. He looks at you a little grimly. "This is your idea. I will support you either way you go. However, if you take too much time, you could cost the company money – either in the short term with employees and our ability to rebound – or in the longer term."

You walk back to your office. Your #1 Strategy has been developed, and you know the path you want to take. There are risks with both approaches. What do you do?

- It's time to move to the next step for this to work. - Go to page 46
- It would be nice to go in order of the steps, but you are focused on reality and what needs to be done - Go to page 69

You have made the decision – the best thing you can do for your organization is to develop each of the steps in the 5 Part Pivot Plan. Pivot for the company while the "pivot is hot." You've decided on focusing on four areas – Process, Supply Chain, R&D (research & development), and Digital Transformation, that will help your organization break out of the industry "pack."

However, you can't go anywhere without your people. You begin to look at your #2 People checklist (Appendix B - #2 People Checklist). Whew... there's a lot of stuff on this list. There's no way you can cover everything. There are so many people! Plus... you have a team of 10... but there's a lot more in the organization. Maybe there's a lighter version of this. Perhaps you don't need to get into all the details, but get the "Pareto 80-20" and do the majority of it.. or at least the highlights.

Or... maybe you bite the bullet and just do it. It's been a while since anyone has looked at the workforce. Now's a good time as any.

- A cursory review of the employee interactions is plenty. You have to look at the big picture - Go to page 47
- It would be nice to look at a high level, but you're suspicious that more time is needed to understand the people. You need to be thorough. - Go to page 49

With the CFO's, Greg comments ringing in your head, you realize you don't have time to waste on a full deep dive into the "people pivot performance." It's already apparent what's happening – the people can be seen walking around – some like business is usual, some like they are waiting for the sky to fall. (To be fair.. some of them were acting like Chicken Little before!)

With a mindset of getting the majority of "the important stuff" – you gather the information from the checklist you can. You do interviews with your team and get the managers of other teams to do them, send surveys, or emails – as much as you can. You end up getting decent data... or at least it appears. Nothing looks out of place... nothing seems out of the ordinary.

Suddenly, you feel a bit uneasy. The information is useful... not great. You realize there may be a problem with *not* talking to the "difficult" people and managers. Could you be leaving out a whole group of people that would fight any pivot or change management project? Regardless of how it would affect them? The Pivot Strategy plan you developed a little while ago may not seem as well-rounded as you first perceived?

Your personal life starts up again, and the commitments that you were required to do before are back. Your workload is now calling for your evenings and weekends. Suddenly it seemed like what was a great idea just a few days and weeks back – is overwhelming – and without good results.

What do you do?

- It's going in the right direction, keep it going... - Go to page 48
- Maybe you should follow your hunch and try again, even if it means starting over... - Go to page 49

If something is too good to be true, it probably is.

You start talking to HR about your results. The managers are upset that you were playing in "their territory" without talking to them. Unfortunately, that pretty much shuts them down to listen to anything else you have to say... even the good stuff.

You persevere, however, and continue to work with some of your friends in other departments. You show them ways they can make an impact on their teams – immediately – but it takes some work.

"Yeah yeah," one of them said to you. "Sounds great on paper, but we have to do, you know, real work. We have to hit these numbers since we're so far off of sales for the year. We don't have time to play 'help the employee with every little problem' so they don't get their feelings hurt."

After a few of these, you give up. Why did you start this again? You're not sure...

- Go to page 12

You realize that *not* doing a deep dive into "#2 People Pivot performance" would be a waste a time of even doing the project. Yes, it will take more time than you want, and you'll probably curse yourself several times during the project – but it hasn't been done, well, perhaps ever. And you feel – no, you *know*, in your gut, you're right. You just have to prove it.

You painstakingly take the time to get nearly all of the information from almost all the employees. You have managers that do a great job gathering the information and others you have to help. After a while, you realize that there are some significant trends, and have collected enough information to help the organization.

You also start getting feedback from several managers that they learned a significant amount from talking to their people about the questions you asked them. They were shocked to find out how many people were affected, and more importantly, the ways in which they were concerned. Some people acted like nothing at all had happened – but really, their worlds had imploded for various reasons. Others, who frequently were deemed some version of "melodramatic," became calm and resolute in their post-crisis views. They were ready to help, and a few were recommended to your team.

Go to the next page.

The information came in... and came in... and came in. You felt you had more than you knew what to do with it. The trends you saw earlier continued to manifest themselves in several ways. You saw apparent themes. Many overlapped - or at least did not conflict – with your #1 Strategy plan you built earlier.

You thought through the comparison and started realizing that you needed to make some decisions. Something needed to be done – some action needed to happen, or you may lose your momentum for the pivot. You had the data. Did you need to spend the time to deep dive and get into the Analysis? Wouldn't it be easier to just move forward with developing the Action plan? You had the two major components – the Strategy and People Plans – wasn't it time for Action?

- It's time for the next step. Again.. it may be time-consuming, but how else are you going to understand the data? - Go to page 51
- Yes... you've learned all you can about Strategy and what's best for your people. It's time to take action. Now. - Go to page 66

An organization only gets a few times to do it right. The first time is (duh) the first time they set up: their structure, their processes, their culture, their people. Most times, organizations are good at some, but not all, of these elements. The organization tends to thrive in the areas the leaders excel in. If the CEO is an operations guru, the business thrives on process & procedure. "People, Process Results! These are the dimensions of success!" You can remember hearing him say. They may have the ability to grow but may struggle in areas of communication, culture, or working with customers.

However, a company led by technical leaders, such as a software, a technology, or a manufactured/engineered product, can find itself mired in the details and almost palpable to the day to day struggles such as growth, standardization, and development.

Such examples are what typically happens within the first few months or years of an organization's life. Some of them become 'death of a thousand paper cuts' – and slowly kill the organization from within. Some are challenges that persistent leaders typically overcome, but not without a struggle. Sometimes that struggle is a 'kick in the pants' problem – such as a blow to the industry, a loss of key leaders, or a severe change in access to resources or customers.

When that happens, a pivot or comeback plan can occur. Still, to thoroughly do one that is successful, that works, is rare. It is hard to have the time, money, and talent to do so.

So... when you were allowed to do it, you knew what gift you had been given. And you were not going to squander it.

Go to page 52

You begin your analysis of the materials. You look at the data from your #1 Strategy… and #2 People … and put it together, using #3 Analysis. You look at the comparison models and information that are out there – and you review the most significant issues in strategy. At a high level, you look at three areas from the analysis:

1. Organization Structure – allowing for three of the five departments to have greater roles so that they can have a greater impact on the customer
2. Leadership by Teams – although there will be leaders by title, there should also be leaders in the teams; these individuals and teams will have specific goals that are aligned with the updated Strategy
3. Innovation 102 - this program will formalize a process that was a one-off before. It will engage in more creation from the teams and fund the next wave of opportunity for the company

There are several others, but based on the repeat information in your #1 Strategy and #2 People results, you look at the opportunities here.

Your boss, John, comes in. "It's been weeks. What are you doing? We don't have time for all of this."

You share the plan with him. You tell him you need another week or so to put the plan together, get the final buy-in, and run with it.

"No," he says. You don't have it. The Q3 numbers are in, and they are not good.

Go to the next page.

What do you say next?

- "This will work. You've given me this far, give me until next week. I will put my job on the line; we are almost there." - Go to page 54
- "I understand. I think this is a great opportunity lost if we stop now. How about I give you a quick plan tomorrow, and we at least get some bang for our buck for the time spent?" - Go to page 63

It was a risky move. You are gambling with your organization's time, which is costing precious money – by using resources. There are other organizations, other industries – that are failing because of this crisis. Much like 9/11 changed the way everyone sees Air Travel. This Crisis is going to impact the future of everything from movie theaters to commuting. No industry is safe. Definitely not yours.

You have a short period to make this work, sell it, and move on. You rely on your skills in project management (both experienced and creative) and ask your friend Stephanie for some more advice on how to put the pieces together (See Appendix D - #4 Action Plan Checklist). You share the plan with a few other managers as well as your team members for feedback.

You do this for several reasons. One – this is where the rubber hits the road – you have to get it right. To make a comeback – you have to get feedback from others on corners you may not have looked around. As much as you rely on your gut, you know that there are areas you could be blinded by, biases you could have.

You find a few areas just like that. A few that made sense for you – but not for individuals that will have to carry out that part of the Pivot plan. You are doing both a Comeback (from a low point in sales and revenue for your organization) and a Pivot (changing the way you do business) – and you need to get as much in the right direction as you can.

Two days later, you are presenting your plan, with timeline and Action steps, to the leadership team. They give you the green light with the caveat. Go now. Go NOW! Every day is a day you lose – to the competition, to the way people choose to do business.

Go to the next page.

You look back at your 5-Piece Pivot Plan. There's another step, but it seems no one in the organization has time for it. Do you?

- Yes – It may make your skin crawl a little to slow the process down when you're ready to go – but there's a reason this step is in there. - Go to page 56

- No – It's time to implement and push the program out. You may risk losing the organization's window for Comeback if you don't. - Go to page 61

If you're not going to do something the way it should be done, then don't do it at all. The leadership is putting pressure on you to get this done so you can see some results. While you don't have the mantra, "you can't hurry greatness" – you know that a few more steps could potentially be the difference from hitting a double and a home run. Just a little more to go.

So... you get to work with a few members of the organization that have now taken an interest in the 5-Piece Pivot Plan and focus on Appendix E - #5 Accountability Checklist. Typically, you're someone who, once you have enough information, you want to jump in and get into the action, to deliver results. You've been told that you're a hammer, and you see everything as a nail – meaning you want to solve problems and fix the thing. (You've realized at some point in this you think in a lot of analogies. Hmmm... is that a good thing? You'll have to figure it out. Not right now, though)

You work through the 5W and 1H Accountability checklist – and realize how much would NOT have been reviewed and checked if you hadn't done it. You read that Accountability is one of two reasons why many leaders struggle to get the job done (Communication being the other one) – and you understand why.

It's great to have a plan, to have the knowledge, to know where you're going. But if the teams don't follow – for whatever reasons – they don't want to, they have no incentive, or their feet aren't held to the fire when they *don't* do what they are supposed to... (see.. another analogy!)...

You look up, startled at your realization. It is now obviously. When they aren't held accountable – then you are on "the road to you know where.... Even if it is paved with good intentions." You're not going there. You're getting it done.

Go to page 57

And you are getting it done. Although the current quarter wraps up in less time than you need to show the results, the next quarter begins creeping up. Week by week, your numbers start to come in. The leadership team's buy-in, and subsequent viewpoint on the individual groups – the way the teams interact with the customers, with each other – has helped pushed the changes through their departments, creating slow acceptance of "The New Normal" in your organization.

Individuals are given more of what they want – and the leadership teams begin to clearly communicate the *why* for the areas they want – but they can't have (example – cash flow issues, capital funding, not enough space in the building, etc.).

At the end of the next quarter, the 5-piece pivot plan has been wildly accepted as a success. You've not only helped your company out of a difficult situation – you may have helped it find a path forward that will allow them to not only thrive – but grow for years to come.

You've already starting to get asked what's next. How are you going to help the organization get to the next step. You start thinking about a trajectory plan. How will you grow and scale in double or triple the capacity and revenue? What would that look like? Your mind starts reeling with the possibilities.

Go to the next page.

In the middle of your daydream (is it a dream?), your boss, John, comes to your office and sits down in front of your desk with a silly grin. "I'm proud of you. You took some risks – some that I was not willing to take. You believed in the 5-piece pivot plan – and made believers out of us. I want to get your name out there –let people know what you did. What do you think?

- This is a big deal.. not just for you but everyone! Let's share the results. - Go to page 59
- It's important, but you don't need that. A simple, quiet success is ok. - Go to page 60

You say, almost shyly, "John, I appreciate it. I do think I worked hard – it was a risk – but it wasn't just me. There are many people – both on my team, and other teams – that stuck their neck out there too. They invested early in the 5-Piece Pivot plan – and they didn't have to. They could have gone about their days, collecting their paychecks. But they didn't. They tried something new – and it paid off. We didn't know it would.. especially in the beginning." You continue. "I'd love to celebrate… for them."

"Done!" John slaps the sides of his chair as he stands up. "On Friday – we'll have a Comeback Celebration. I want people to know what your team did. Put together a few slides that we can rotate through a simple slide show in the background. I want you to talk for 5 minutes about the plan – and make some suggestions on how others can start doing this in a smaller term. How could they do it within their teams? Maybe not on such a grand scale, but still in this method?"

You slightly grimace at the additional work he just gave you ("No good deed goes unpunished!") – but you laugh it off quickly. This is the *right* kind of work – it's a reward in itself.

"You got it, boss," you say.

"Oh, one more thing… " he turns around. "Enjoy the rest of the week.. and on Monday, you're in charge of the Trajectory Plan. We are looking at a Growth Plan, and what got us to here will NOT get us there. It will NOT get us to the next step for our organization. We need some new eyes on the approach, and I put your name on the team. So get ready." And just like that, he walks off.

You spin around in your chair as you realize what's just been said. One adventure may have just ended… but it looks like your next one at work is just beginning.

"I appreciate that John, I do," you start. "I'm ok with just a thank you... and maybe having some time to continue to cultivate the teams – not just to hold them accountable but to help them celebrate their successes too."

He nods. "Of course... I get that about you. Take the rest of the week to walk around and see the impact of your 5-Piece Pivot plan. You've helped people think out of the box. Now... don't get a big head. You were in a good place to make a change like that. We were coming back from a crisis. We needed a win. You found one – it was different, but not so radical people couldn't relate."

He stands up as he walks out of the office. "You did well. Thank you. Take the week to wrap things up and get them going as much on auto-pilot as you can. Next week, you start our Trajectory Plan."

<End>

It's ok – the last step in the 5 Piece Pivot Plan is just the Accountability piece. You'll hold them accountable as much as needed because you'll be there. You're living, eating, and breathing this daily now. You don't have time for much else anyway, and the extra steps in Accountability will just slow you down, trying to make sense of it.

You implement it immediately. You set out on the communication plan. The leadership shares the message as you set it up for them – so their teams get it and know the boss is in charge (or.. at least has some buy into the concepts). Things start happening.

The organization slowly moves. Not as fast as you'd like, and not as quickly as you projected, but over the next several weeks, it starts changing. The End of Quarter (EOQ) numbers are in, and they aren't so dire. You get a pat on the back from your boss, John, and several others, and you move on with your work.

- Go to page 73

You have gone <u>SO</u> much further than you ever thought you would do with the 5 Piece Pivot Plan. Your organization took a good look at the Strategy – how to look at it going forward and what will change.

Even better – you had time to deep dive the People side – what are the key areas that align with the organization, to better coincide with the capabilities – and those that didn't. You (and the organization) learned a lot about some of the areas you didn't even know had strengths in… and you're now using it (well, some of it).

And… if you're honest, the experience itself will be something you will remember for a long time. In a way, you feel like you've Pivoted your own life. You had considered changing companies, going back to school, or just quitting. And now, you've (mostly) completed a Pivot Plan.

Who knows what will happen next.

Curiosity may have killed the cat, but not today. You want to exercise all of the options of the 5-piece pivot plan, and you wanted to do this anyway. Your friend Stephanie, the Operations consultant, had told you this – NOT having an accountability plan – was the #1 reason that most process improvements didn't work.

At a high level – the pivot plan is a process improvement plan – you're trying to improve a process. You're just trying to do it in a significant way. You're pivoting the very nature of the organization's business.

You've come too far to stop now.

- Go to page 56

He grimaces as he gets up. "You have until tomorrow."

You look back at your work, a little sadly. This happens a lot – you get a great idea, a great solution or product.. and then life (or job, or a project) sets in.

You work through the late afternoon and into the evening. You take a look at #4 Action Plan and #5 Accountability, and incorporate some of those steps in your notes, but know it will not be as good as it could have been. However, you're not quite sure it would all work anyway. Even if you got the approval, you've never done something like this before. You're a leader without a lot of experience. Your plate is full already. You're not even sure it would be rewarding to complete this anyway. At best, you'll get a pat on the back…. At worst… you could lose the company money, and potentially get fired.

When presenting to your boss, John, and these thoughts ring in your mind. In the end, he says, "You have me between a rock and a hard place. I see the opportunity... but we don't have the resources. Still – you've been somewhat scrappy with your ideas and resources so far, so I'll leave it to you. It's your choices".

What do you do next?

- Move forward on the shortened, modified plan. It's a lot safer, and it's in your wheelhouse. You know you can succeed. And get to where you want to go next. - Go to page 65
- Go for it. Take the chance. Throw the Hail Mary. Even if you fail, you need to know. - Go to page 66

You take what you have, appreciate it for what it is – and run with it.

You ask for and are granted, time to share your results with the teams. The leadership team likes your strategy comparisons. The HR team likes the people analysis and wants to use some of your work for a leadership development program for new and especially front-line leaders. Some of the other managers use some of your recommendations – focusing on timeline & processes (such as meetings and who should be in them) and best practices from other industries (such as job playbooks, weekly "Dashboard" metric reviews for teams and "Ask the Manager" Employee boards) to align metrics and rewards with strategies, but that is as far it goes.

Still - you were glad to have had the opportunity to get through the steps of the 5-piece pivot plan. Although it didn't ultimately work for your organization this time, you now have a better understanding of how to look at problems in the future and break them down to pieces. How to get from

Strategic → Tactical ….

Organization → Individual …

Goals → Action.

You'll continue using this Pivot Plan. You've learned that comebacks can happen every day – in all shapes and sizes.

It's time for action. You've already spent weeks gathering the data. You have a good strategy. You have the understanding of the people – what they want, what they don't. You know the three key elements the team/ organization needs to pivot.

Now... you just need to do it.

You review your Action Plan Checklist (Appendix D - #4 Action Plan Checklist) – and focus on the BIG bang for your buck. You need to grow sales. Quickly. You need to move the needle. You sell the action plan quickly and get to work on the results

However, over the next few weeks, you begin seeing why Step #3 – Analysis, was so important. There were complete groups you overlooked. Areas that affected the customers were not addressed – but would have been if you'd put the first two steps in the Pivot Plan together.

If you'd spent the time developing those together in Step #3, the comparison would have brought several issues and conflicts to life. What ended up being suitable for the organization was NOT good for the employees – and so incentives were NOT aligned, and rewards (and punishments) did not match the results. People just stopped working, in some cases – in important areas.

It wasn't all bad. There were some areas within the Pivot – especially the top item – that was seeing some results. Your boss, John, comes to you after more of the results emerge. "You did well in a few areas, but some of these areas have to go. We have to pull the plug – and either go back to the way it was or cut our losses which would be the time and money we've already spent on this)."

Go to the next page.

He continues, "We can keep the areas that are completely working... or pick a different path and do something else...." He pauses and considers it. "If we do something else – you need to be clear in what you're going to do differently.

Cause → Effect → Impact.

How will you be able to get it done – to the benefit of the team and the organization? Can it be done? You've got some success under your belt – don't waste it".

What do you do?

- You've got this far. The EOQ (End of the quarter) numbers are looming. You want to make sure what works sticks, then see what happens. - Go to page 68
- Try again. There may be something that you missed. You don't feel like missing it. Not today. - Go to page 51

You decide that the right thing to do is to take a break. Not... stop... But, make sure that what is already in place is already working. You remember reading about change management – if you introduce too many variables, too many unknowns at one time – you could overload the system – in this case – the people and the very structure you're trying so hard to pivot.

Over the next few weeks and months, things start to settle down. Some of the approaches work... some, you come to realize, begin going back to their original state. Possibly because there were not a lot of control measures in place (you know that later, after looking up #5 – Accountability, and seeing how you could have done a few things differently), or possibly because the crisis wasn't as bad, and your ideas were standing in the way of getting the job done the way they want.

You've developed a basic plan that helped the organization with the post-crisis recovery. Is it a comeback plan? Well... it's got some merit. People are looking at the way they work in a different light. For example – requiring 15 people in a meeting from the same three departments no longer happens – now, only five or six of the essential people show up and then report back to their teams on the critical items.

Still... you're not quite sure if you can differentiate if that was the comeback plan – or people's natural reaction to the crisis. You've come to realize people are fairly resilient. Probably more than you gave them credit for, maybe they could have done more with an absolute comeback plan.

Guess you'll have to wait until the next crisis to find out.

It's too risky to waste time here. The organization is already behind the eight ball. You've lost a lot in cash flows, sales are below the charts, and senior leadership is looking daily at the not-so-off chance of getting rid of people.

You realize you are in a medium to higher risk industry – one that could see some shakeup in the upcoming months. You review the information (Appendix D - #4 Action Plan Checklist) to review and build and Action plan – **intending** to get **results. Now**.

You talk to several groups in your organization. They have already heard about the changes you want to make, and they are wary. Still, you have the CFO's backing, and that goes a long way. You are tripped up several times by the fact that you did not want a deep dive into the people/ impact aspect of it (heck, you didn't dive into it at all) – but you just didn't have the time to do that.

The change is substantial. You work with multiple groups, including HR, who has someone trained in change management. But this is the right path, you know it. Change is hard. It sounds clique, but it's the truth.

You develop the details. The changes will happen for the next three months. It won't be a lot of time, but you need to pivot the business, change the culture, and bring everyone over to the other side of the "bridge." It's a fast-moving plan.

You'll know when you've succeeded when you don't fail (ok.. that may be a bit dramatic). You know you've succeeded when the organization's cash flow and sales begin to take a turn beyond what it's seen the last few weeks – and at least match or beat what you knew before the crisis. You know there are some outside factors, but your plan is the main one in play.

Go to the next page.

However, when you present it to the leadership again, you get a lukewarm response. They are for it, but they don't have the bandwidth to support you. The CFO says – "you've got this" and leaves it at that. Your boss, John, is a supporter, but he won't be of help with the rest of the pivot items you have within the organization. You don't know the people or culture – you didn't have time to understand it (and you're not sure if it mattered) – but now you're at a crossroads. You're getting frustrated with the "on-again/ off-again" approach of this business.

- Do you take the risk – implement the plan – because you think they care? - Go to page 71
- Do you hesitate, gather more information – because you're not convinced this will work – and that means you could be out of a job? - Go to page 72

Ready or not, here you come.

You decide that there's merit in the program you've set up. You've fleshed out your Action Plan enough – with your boss, your peers, and the team. You've reached a few others in the organization, and although some are resistant – you know some of that is resistant to change.

The program is different. There are areas people have never seen. There is an organizational change that helps align the people that need to make decisions with the actual choices themselves. Before it was a matrix approach that was good for getting information out, but not for making decisions – at least not for your particular organization.

You also realign how sales and revenue numbers are rewarded. Not just for the sales and marketing team – but all teams. You look at the metrics and better align the programs. Some people will not receive a large a compensation bonus as before Covid-19. Still, others recognize the work rewarded is the right thing for the organization (not just an individual).

You do a cursory glance at the strategy and people suggestions of the 5 Piece Pivot Plan program after the rollout – and realize there were some elements you really could have benefitted from. Your team struggles with the buy-in. There's a large group of individuals you overlooked because you had no idea their issues even existed.

You have some successes and some failures. Although you hope there never is a next time with a crisis on this scale, you think you would prefer to do all the steps in the 5-Piece Pivot Plan for a more understood, well-rounded approach to the crisis and subsequent action plan.

You hope there's never a next time .. but if there is, you'll be ready.

Yeah… they say that "the path to you know where is paved with good intentions." You have good intentions.. but in a place like this, is it worth it?

You hesitate. The action plan is there. Maybe… maybe you'll do a few elements in your group – see how they take to it. You roll out parts of the action plan – the ones dealing with the team – how to get them to do things, standardizing some of the processes that have never been standardized—working on communication that has never been done before.

You do the rollout with your team. Weeks go by. It goes….., ok. Some of the areas work (Hmmm.. maybe you should look into the 5 Piece Pivot Plan step on Accountability? (Appendix E) Some of the areas seem to falter because of the individuals involved (would the 5 Piece Pivot Plan step on People help here?).

You're starting to feel burnt out on this. On the one hand – communication has improved, and there's less conflict in the group. On the other – the processes didn't work. You're not sure why. There's a part of you that's curious if it did. What would it look like? Do you have the ability to make it happen – even for your team?

Do you find out?

- Yes – You want to know you tried to make it happen. You think there's a chance for Pivot, even if it's a lot of work. You've got to try. - Go to page 46
- No – You've had your say, and made some moves. No reason to rock the boat further. You prefer to keep your job.. Thank you. - Go to page 13

A month later, your boss, John, comes to your office with an angry expression. *Uh oh.* You think He usually doesn't "do" angry. He's normally a happy-go-lucky kind of guy.

"Why didn't you check the three areas that we pivoted last month?" He asks.

"What do you mean? They were fine…" You're thinking hard as you hesitate in your response. You haven't checked several areas of the Pivot Plan in weeks – they were running so well.

"Yeah, well… you better check again. Only one out of the five-team are still doing it that way. Everyone else has reverted. Maybe we don't need the Pivot. Maybe we just needed that boost. But you should have done a better job of checking up on them…"

You think back to the last step in the Pivot Plan. That could solve it, but do you need to? The numbers are good enough, and you could make it worse overall if you push the issue now. Still, there's a part of you that's curious…

- Stay as it is, don't rock boat. - Go to page 62
- Consider the options. - Go to page 63

Epilogue – 5-Piece Pivot Plan (5-3P) Overview

The 5-Piece Pivot Plan (5-3P) is a framework that helps leaders and small business owners look at their teams, better understand their (true) challenges, and develop a new strategy going forward – that is beneficial to BOTH the organization and its employees. It does this by explicitly focusing on the crisis/ major change that occurred (such as COVID in 2020, a merger of two different organizations, an accidental release of a reorg that was premature and incomplete).

Questions to answer: How can you solve your old problems…. In a new way? How can you get ahead of competitors? How can you ramp up faster with the resources you currently have?

Diving further, specific questions answer focus areas based on the current situation of the organization and employees. Each represents a different "piece" of the plan. Each area should be addressed to some extent to ensure a full understanding of the "Pivot" plan is developed.

At a glance:

Piece	Question
1	What does the team/ organization need? To survive? To thrive?
2	What does the individual /employee want? What are needs not being met?
3	What are the differences between the organization and the individual? What is not obvious between the two that is causing the discrepancy?
4	How do you get it done and make it happen... so both the organization and employee are successful long term? How do you level the playing field in your organization?
5	How can you make these changes stick? How do you ensure the good parts stay and the bad go away?

Parts of the Pivot Plan & Questions to consider:

- #1 Strategy – What is essential to the organization? (Really important... now? Not just because it was important months ago). What has changed? - This area will focus on individuals strategies of the company. The mantra "what got you here will not get you there" will help define the future of a comeback.

- #2 People – Who are they... now? What do they represent – to themselves and the company? How did the incidents from the last few months affect them? People change during a crisis, internally and externally, as well as personally and professionally. Being aware of those changes and impacts will not only improve them but could also benefit the organization if correctly harnessed.

- #3 – Organization/ Individual – comparison – What aligns? What may be in conflict? Which elements are most important? An analysis is required to understand the gaps – what is different? How can you resolve those differences? This can require some out of the box thinking as well as opportunities for others in the organization to have a voice (such as junior personnel and inexperienced people in specific roles)

- #4 – Action plan – There's the first iteration before you start (what you're doing now) – but what does it look like now that you have the info? What are the critical priorities? What is not so important? In this step- explanation and communication are key. You are clearly sharing the "why" to the organization or team. Why are you doing what you're doing? Share information beyond what they are expected to know in their roles, helping them understand the bigger picture.

- #5 – Accountability - How to make it stick? How do you get long term buy in to complete the pivot? Perhaps the most critical piece of the plan and the least utilized – holding people, teams, and the organization accountable for their piece of the pie is the KEY to long-lasting results. Developing a plan to carry out AND follow up will continue to grow successfully in the future.

Appendix A - #1 - Strategy

<u>Strategy & Pivot – An introduction</u>

The first step in the 5-piece pivot plan (5-3P) is strategy. An organization cannot function without a sound strategy as a framework and a baseline. However, during a crisis, the strategies that you used before may not work now. You may have to look at other options, other frameworks – different ways to pivot.

The below framework is a "Strategy checklist" for coming back from a crisis. Challenge yourself and your team's way of thinking by answering the questions – not as you've done it before but as an "ideal" way of doing the thing for your team. Be open to outside of the box approaches.

<u>Strategy & Pivot – A checklist</u>

Note: There are two methods for the framework – You can use Questions 1-6 to look at resources needed for this section. The table can be used as a "quick look" into the areas you want to focus on and why. Feel free to use them together or separately as appropriate for your team or organization.

1. Gather resources – what will you need to review?
    a. Employees – analytical ability, time allocation
    b. Resources – meeting time, space, brainstorm sessions

2. Get buy-in – Who do you need to support the plan?

3. Past plan –What were the prior Strategies and Goals? What were the (most) important priorities before? (in the last year?)

4. New plan – Updated important, strategies & goals. Where will the industry be going? What will need to change?
    a. Note: this may require brainstorming – for the most part, little to no knowledge/ research is known in this area. For example – will your workforce work more from home after the amount of WFH (work from home) they did? Could you reduce the real estate you rent because of it? ...etc...
    b. Resources: Recommend gathering open-minded individuals from various experiences, strengths, and levels of your organization for maximum effectiveness
    c. Everything works! Do not close an idea until all are on the table
    d. Specific Strategy Recommendations: See Suggestions & References

5. Feasibility – Reviewing your lists from #3 and #4 – how do they compare. <u>What is most relevant to your company moving forward?</u>

    a. The first answer: Survival. How will you survive?

    b. Next: Thrive. What areas in your "New Plan" help you grow and thrive?

6. Develop your new strategy based on the information provided above. Focus brainstorming sessions on areas of opportunities: can you reduce in areas that is adding wasteful processes, can you add value to customers? How can you be different? How can you take advantage of current technology?

Strategy & Pivot – Framework Questions

Item	Questions	Actions/ Answers
A - Organization's (org) strategy – before the crisis		
B- Org's goals – before the crisis (if different than item A above)		
C- Team's strategy – before the crisis		
D - Team's goals – before the crisis		
A & B – Organization - What will not work in A & B... what has changed with the crisis?		
C & D – Organization - What will not work in C&D ... what has changed with the crisis?		

E - Feasibility – What is most important to your organization/ team going forward? (profit, growth, employees, etc.)		
Out of the box – ideas – how can you accomplish E?		
Output – Strategic ideas moving forward (take this to the next Section). Note – does not need to be fully completed/ actionable at this step		

Strategic Ideas → Tactical Actions

Below is a collection of ideas that could be applied in groups and organizations. Take note they should not all be applied (at the same time), and many of them may not work with your particular group/organization. Make sure to spend some time understanding the dynamics of your group, the culture, and the current state (of the business cycle, crisis impact, mindset, etc.).

Communication

- What was the current communication strategy before the crisis? Be honest – what worked and what didn't?
    o If you have not had a chance to evaluate – then ask for feedback from various individuals. Ask such questions as "What are our current goals? What is important for our company? Where do you think we should be headed?"
    o If they cannot answer those questions, you need to develop your communication strategy
- Get the message out. Everyone knows the organization went through the crisis. They do <u>not</u> understand what's being done. You need to get that message out – the sooner, the better.
    o Err on the side of over-communication. You want them to know where you stand – and where you are going.

Meetings & WFH

- WFH – Work from home. After months of working from home – how much more do you need?
    o More – when things go back to normal – do your people want more or less? Can you give it to them? Don't just go back to "how things were" if 1)

people enjoyed WFH 2) the work got done. Period. Find ways to help people do more of what they want. Such as WFH.

- o Less – if your culture encourages face to face interaction – allow it to happen! Listen to your people, and understand what drives their maximum productivity (see Appendix B - #2 People Checklist for more ideas)
- WFH Strategy Successes – Tried and correct methods for maximum productivity at home
  - o Set a time for 50 minutes – Walk around at least 5 minutes – put a load of clothes in the washer, clean your room. You would do this at work anyway (get coffee, talk to a co-worker)
  - o Functional team meeting – Give yourself (and the team) something to look forward to. Keep the meeting short – do NOT make it 15 or 30 minutes because that's easy. Allow for "chat" – get a few an icebreaker questions (such as "what was the worst birthday present you've ever received?" to get the conversation started
- WFH – Get rid of office space?
  - o This is a longer-term strategy – Do you need all the space that you currently have? Could you re-define how your people do their work in the office – and save some valuable long term costs?
  - o Additional costs – savings on commuting (including $/ mile for travelers), office supplies,

Risk Management

- IT infrastructure
  - o What does your current IT management system look like? How often is it revisited?

- o How did the crisis change the way the organization looked at software/ hardware? Would you be able to manage another crisis?
- o What is the maintenance/ replacement plan for what you critically need? (Such as laptops, webcams, shared IT resources) What about the areas you don't critically need – but they are still important?
- Contingency plan
  - o Do you have one?
  - o If one person in your office immediately left tomorrow – what challenges would fall to your organization or team?
  - o Playbook – Create a playbook for all critical areas of the organization. This allows for backup of any area. This does not have to include every step an individual performs, but it should reference the key areas, processes, work and people needed to complete the job

Revenue & Growth

- Recovering revenue quickly – The SHAPE model
  - o Startup Mindset
  - o Human at the Core
  - o Acceleration of digital, tech, analytics,
  - o Purpose-driven customer playbook
  - o Ecosystems & adaptability

Additional Strategic Resources

- See also References – Strategy – for more articles on Strategic Comeback Plans
- The Wise Advocate (Kleiner, Thomson & Schwartz, 2019)
  - o Decision Challenge: Moment of Choice

- Transactional – You solve the problem, or make the deal, focusing on what people want. You are expedient and know how to get things done.
- Strategic – You focus NOT on what just people want, but on who they are, and what is best in the long run. You listen to your inner Wise Advocate.

Appendix B - #2 People Checklist

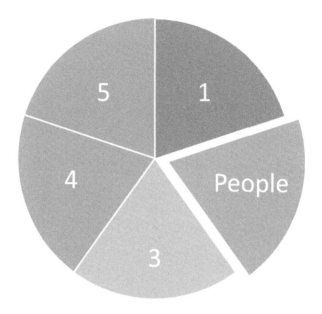

1. List the employees on your team
2. Who are they? Key motivators, personality, career anchors, MBTI
3. New skills? Did any of them gain a new skill during the time of separation? Anything beneficial to the organization – *even if it's not to their specific job description?*
    a. Look at options for Career Engagement (Prisant-Lesko 2015)
4. How did the last few months affect them?
    a. There are multiple ways to approach this. You can use 1x1s, assessments, etc. Your goal is to find out how they were impacted. Are they ready to be back at work? Hesitant? Missing certain things? Were they worried about other things that are not entirely "back to

normal"? Have they accepted a new way of thinking that may affect how they did their job before?

    b. In the end, you should know your employees the best. The list above has suggestions on approaches.

5. What do they want now? Similar to the #1 Strategy approach – if the information in steps 1-3 is "before," then what does the "new" or "after" look like? What is their three-month, one year, three year plan look like?

6. How different is the "before" and "after" plan of the individuals?

Appendix C - #3 Analysis Checklist

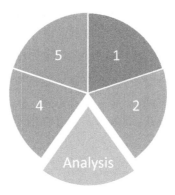

Analysis - How do you put the pieces together?

Adapted from: *Go Beyond the Job Description,* Prisant-Lesko (2018)

You have a lot of data, probably spread around many areas: in a Word document here, in an e-mail there, maybe even on a few scraps of paper. It's now time to put all of that together to understand what you have, find the trends, and make use of it to move forward on fully engaging the talent you have in your organization.

Getting started: Comparing what you already have: Strategy & People

You have already collected some data—either quantitative (numeric in some way) or qualitative (primarily words, numbers that don't add, such as interviews). How much data do you need to have at this point? That's a good question, but you don't need to have a finite answer (or a tremendous amount of data). You will need data to support the transition—to make it relatively relevant. Have 50 employees? Interviewing 10 percent of the workforce is only five people. It is not much of a sample size, but you may be able to conduct a combination of assessments and short interviews to obtain enough data. Have a CEO or leader who needs lots of numbers? You will probably have to gather a bit more data to satisfy their desire for the facts through data.

The goal of reading the results from #1 Strategy and #2 People is to make sense of a mountain of data. Whether the activity is called "research" or "trend analysis," you are trying to parse the results and understand the information in front of you.

Trend analysis is the ability to take somewhat unrelated data and find the ways they are related—in a way that is important to you, your research, and your ultimate goals. In true academic research, most results are unknown. Hence, we develop hypotheses to direct our research toward an outcome.

Likewise, you don't know the results until you analyze the data, but you do know what you'd like them to look like. You want the results to offer a clear outcome on whether or not we're on the right path to developing a more productive organization. You want to have a more engaged workforce. You'd like to streamline your people processes or give people more time back in their day. All of these things are the goals—and as in academic research—you focus on these goals, your "research question," when digging into the data. Focus on the goal, what you're trying to resolve, and it will help you align your benchmark metrics to your final (successful!) results.

Finding the trends

Quantitative versus Qualitative

With quantitative data, you are looking for numbers – ratios, cash flows, ROI's, for example. Qualitative data is looking at the data for *words* .. and their relative meaning. Qualitative data can be somewhat more cumbersome than its quantitative brother. —. In contrast, quantitative is black-and-white numbers (it either is 22, or it's not), qualitative data tends to be relative, in the eye of the beholder.

There is significant literature on methods for doing analysis, so below are several recommendations for you to do your own that focuses on the analysis of the information in the previous sections:

Analysis Suggestions:

Organization/ Individual gap analysis

-   Simple comparison – What was the strategy for the organization/team / individuals before? What is it now? How do they compare, and how can change occur?
-   Organizational priorities vs. Employee Drive-In comparison of the two – how different are the motivation and priorities than they were before the crisis? How can these differences be resolved?
-   Could a change to innovation, imitation strategy or Cost-minimizing strategy help the organization – even if it was not there before?

Organizational Culture & Future Plans

-   Is the culture of the organization or team in the right place? Should it be part of the evaluation based on the information received?
-   Future plans – where should the company be in 1, 3, 5 years? How different is that from your previous plans? How difficult will it be to get employees to follow these changes?
-   Talent engagement – Do you have the ability to engage further and challenge the talent that is already in the company? Could you engage the skills and push the employees to do things they want to do – but are not being asked to?

Analysis checklist: Turn words from raw data (that you collected previously) into data you can use

1. *Gather all your notes.* Put them in one location.
2. *Organize your notes.* Use your preferred method for organizing your thoughts/work. For me, this is in Excel.

3. *Transfer your notes*. Enter text into columns (for example, in a spreadsheet or table) with labels such as these:
   - Name
   - Position
   - Department/Team (if important)
   - Comment
   - Trend

Analysis: Ideas Toolbox … "Necessity is the mother of invention."

This time is an opportunity to step back. The impact the crisis is having on your team/ organization may be a one time chance to make a difference in your area. Use the suggestions below as food for thought.. are these opportunities for your team?)

It is easy to lead when you know where you want to go… and harder to do it when you have no idea where to go. You have the opportunity to break new ground… and make a lasting impact.

- Pivot Opportunities & Ideas -
  - People
    - People can work from home and still do their job .. just as well
    - Evaluation – should it be based on Incentive – or evaluation now? How are you aligning rewards/ metrics – with strategies & goals?
  - Process
    - Standardizing
    - Simplifying

- o Organization
  - become a virtual org, a boundaryless org
  - "How do you pivot & stay alive and make sure you bring your people along with you?"
- o Office
  - Should you redesign the office? https://www.architecturaldigest.com/story/covid-19-design
  - Should you use different hardware/ software to do the job? https://www.realsimple.com/work-life/technology/best-video-conferencing-options
- o Changes
  - Recommendation: Make changes fast. If you decide to make a move, this is the time to do it.
  - Routine is no longer …routine (make a new one!) – take advantage
  - Question: what do you NOT want to return? (PIVOT that!)

Appendix D - #4 Action Plan Checklist

Excerpt from *"Go Beyond the job description" By Ashley Prisant Lesko*

The dictionary defines an action plan as a "proposed strategy or course of action." After years of managing strategic action plans, I personally believe there is a number of different methods to solve the problem. **The strategy allows for flexibility**. Your action plan should be flexible, but with a specific purpose or goal in mind.

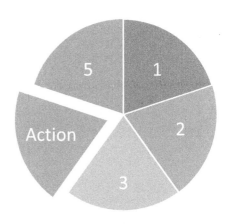

Action Plan: Focus Areas

A simple action plan can be a single table/ spreadsheet for EACH of the goals you want to accomplish – and then columns to show the results/ effects/ tasks/ action to complete. Potential areas could be:

- Goal – (Objective)
- Activities (Tasks) - Specifically what needs to be done
- Location (Where) – If a specific location is important
- Metrics Addressing – Which metric to be measured?
- Success Criteria – How do you know when this task/ goal is successful?
- Timing (Deadline) - For the task to be complete)
- Resources (People) – Who is needed to complete the task
- Resources (Material) – What is needed to complete the task
- Potential Constraints - What could stop you from getting it done by the deadline?

- Priority Level – (Importance Level) – Could be in order of necessity or impact, based on timing or otherwise – to give weight to the task's importance
- Impact (Cost/Savings) – In $/Hours/ other ROI areas that could help define the priority for resources or help explain savings of the project
- Impact (People) – Who will be affected during this task (i.e., software that would be down for 24 hours, part of an office that would need training for 2 hours)
- Marketing – (strategy) How will it be rolled out?

Table D-1 – Action Plan Table

Goal	Task/ Activity	Timing	Metrics Addressing	Success Criteria	Resources - People
Increasing Employee Productivity	Engage at least one specific strength	By the end of 100 days	Employee Productivity/ Capacity	All ten employees in the team will be using one strength outside of job description	All people in team + manager - 2x/ month for 1 hour each

Putting the Action Plan together - Additional questions to consider:

- Communication – Who shares the message? How do you want to motivate them? What is the company culture like? Is it better in a rally? A quiet lunch?
    - The book *Great Game of Business* has excellent recommendations on how to share new information with employees to help them see the bigger picture
- Timing – When will you relay the comeback plan? Does the time of day, week, month, or year make a difference? (Note: There may not be a choice when you get to deliver the message post-crisis, but if you have some flexibility, it may be better to postpone, for example, schools that are out in the summer)
- Points for consideration in putting together your Action Plan
    - How risky is your industry?
    - How much change do you want to make?
    - What stands in your way?
    - How fast can you go?
    - How do you know when you've succeeded?
- Change management – How will the changes/ action plan impact affect the team, group or organization? They may have already been affected so much by the crisis… does that make an impact?
    - Challenge stressors – What happened before, what is happening now – are major impacts. People are impacted in multiple ways – some you don't understand (some you don't want to know). Understand that any new information could be a challenge stressor. Do NOT present new information like a bull in a china shop unless there is NO. OTHER. CHOICE.
- Know who you know. Who is your workforce?
    - What motivates them? Preferably, a more thorough step would be to See #2 – People Checklist. At a minimum,

you must know them as demographic, groups, and cultural mindset.

- Are they Older or younger? Junior or Senior? Experienced or Entry level? Blue or White collar? How do the differences impact them?
- Is your industry at risk? For example – restaurants, funeral parlors, farming – are industries that could be at a unique risk under certain circumstances

- SAY IT the way they understand. It is not about the money to employees – it could be more about <u>getting the buy-in</u>. Remember, you see the obvious reason for this Action Plan – but others do not. You need to bring them along as much as possible.

Action Plan – Potential Tactics

- **Tracking the metrics – building a dashboard**
  - o Excerpt from *"Go Beyond the job description" By Ashley Prisant Lesko*
  - o Goal: Having pertinent, relevant information at your fingertips – when you need it
  - o Type: Quantitative
  - o Ease of use: High Difficulty
  - o Explanation: Perhaps your team has realized they can't be productive because they don't know how well they are doing something – or in the case of one business – they didn't even measure their processes – so they accepted whatever time their employees finished a job. Understanding *what* is important as well as the *how much*, but an additional question is *how does this number relate with what we planned* is even MORE important

- Find the metrics – where will the information come from? What numbers are needed? Where is the source
- Already created or build it? Many dashboards already exist out there – for some, they already have them built into their business with a current software package – they just don't know it. If you think you have it – ask the software team. If you don't – you can create it with something as simple as Excel
- Make it easy – Don't make the dashboard so that you are the only one that can operate it.
- Make it repeatable. AND replicable. Updating or uploading to a dashboard should take no more than 30 seconds to update.
- Make a playbook. As you develop the Dashboard – make sure to write down the directions as you go – so they are fresh, and others can follow your example. You know it best – help them learn it, too.

- Level the field
  - Use *Great Game of Business* tactics to help employees see beyond their own line of work
  - Use Pareto – find the areas on your list for the biggest bang for your buck
  - Use Cialdini, *Influence* and his other book – to Influence people to pivot
  - Learning organization – Are you an organization that naturally changes? Consider adding methods for creating a "learning organization" culture – one that encourages **Failing Forward, Innovating Fast** and **Failing Quickly**

Appendix E - #5 Accountability Checklist

Making it stick… holding them & yourself accountable Leaders must be consistent in two things to secure repeat performances out of their teams – this includes <u>communication</u> and <u>accountability</u> (Prisant Lesko, 2015). A message must be clear to the receiver (not just the one delivering the message) and understood. Its contents (for action, follow-through, next steps, etc.) must have expectations (timeline, consequences) that the recipient of the message understands.

The action requested must be completed. If not, the recipient could:

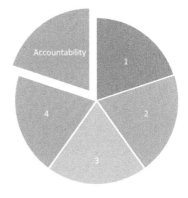

- Be confused about what is expected and when
- Be mad for not having a consistent message
- Push back on future requests
- Refuse to do future actions because the consequence does not matter

Below is a guideline for an accountability checklist to help ensure teams, tasks, or projects stay on track. <u>Key Note:</u> The most important work done in this checklist – is YOUR OWN – it is YOUR follow through – not the work of your team's. They MUST know you will confirm their action is complete (without micro-managing them).

5W's and 1H for Accountability

Item	Questions	Actions/ Answers
Who	Who is ultimately responsible for this job, task, or project?	
Who (Individual)	If it is an individual – list the names and key responsibilities	
Who (Team/ Group)	If it is a team – list the team w/ names and actions. How will you determine who does what actions? Does it matter? If there is a team leader, make sure that person is at the top of the list.	
What	What are they supposed to do? Do they understand? You have to set clear expectations and, making sure to follow up.	
When	Timeline – What is the timeline the action needs to be completed? When should they turn something in – and how should they check-in?	
Where	Where should they go if they make a mistake? Encourage them that it's ok to make mistakes, but they (and you) should communicate problems as soon as they can. It's better NOT to be the senior person with a secret – but a team that resolves quickly.	

Why	Why are we doing this? What happens if we don't? Some individuals will need reassurance. Others will need understanding and information. Make sure this is clear. You won't win over everyone, but you do need some early adopters and key "popular vote" people to continue to support and move the project / change forward	
How	How often to follow up? This depends on the intensity (how often the item occurs or needs to happen) and resistance (how big is the change, how much work is involved). The higher the intensity or resistance, the greater the follow up (daily, weekly, etc.)	

Appendix F- Motivation 101

Motivation can come in all shapes and sizes – but it is the foundation for anyone to do anything. Why do you get up in the morning? Why do you go to work? Why do you make a choice to do something or not? Specifically, to the topics in this book, you are focusing on two areas of motivation:

1. Self-Motivation - How do you get yourself to do something (especially if you don't want to, but know you need to)
2. Motivation of others – How do you motivate your team to do something? To complete a goal? How do you get your boss to agree with the plan you've set up? Or go in a different direction?

Note: Motivation is a broad topic; additional information in the References section.

Self-Motivation Tactics

"Fake it 'til you make it"

You know it needs to be done. You have every reason to get it done. But you don't want to do it. You don't want to be energetic. This tactic helps you get the job done by pretending you're already in the position of completion.

What do you really want?

Many people will do things – even for themselves – because it is comfortable – even if it is causing them pain. Is it a short term pain for long term gain? For example, a two year project or job that will help you springboard your career? If so, change your mindset and focus on the longer-term "why" you're there.

If / then
If I do this, then I will get this (can be carrot or stick). Help yourself understand the effects of your current actions.

Just … Suck it up
Like that vegetable on the plate, you didn't want to eat as a kid – close your eyes, do the task and swallow!

Motivation of others

Career Anchors

Why do people do what they do at work? What are the primary motivators? Why would people turn down a job – that offered more prestige or money? It is because of Career Anchors – the motivational anchors that drive them most at work. There are eight anchors. People tend to have 2-3 primary anchors. Getting to know which ones drive your team can help you motivate them.

Career Anchors – Brief Description
Adapted From: *Career Anchors: The Changing Nature of Careers Self-Assessment* (Schein & Maanen, 2013)

1. Autonomy/Independence- Having Autonomy / Independence as a Career anchor means you prefer to not have organizational constraints of a specific task or function. You would prefer to have less restrictive work requirements, schedules and prefer to have more flexibility.
2. Security / Stability - Priorities for those with Security/ Stability is knowing they will have a place to go to work, at a regular expected time, and receive regular expected pay. You would prefer to give up change in your career or opportunities if it meant a potential for greater risk in your job security.
3. Lifestyle – Those having Lifestyle prefer to focus on the true balance between work and life. They prefer working to live, not

the other way around. It does not mean these individuals are lazy by any means, but have prioritized the balance of work, family and friends and want to do it in their own manner.

4. Technical/ Functional – Individuals who prefer Technical / Functional enjoy being competent in their skill set and prefer that managing others or their independence if it meant they could not demonstrate their expertise. They prefer to grow only that area of expertise.

5. General Managerial – The General Managerial Competence anchor actually derives from three competencies – analytical, interpersonal and emotional competencies. These individuals want to have the "bigger picture", want to achieve the overarching goals, and are stimulated by solving problems, and having high levels of responsibility.

6. Entrepreneurial Creativity – Not only for those choosing to start a business, this anchor is for those that want to develop, build, create something of their own. They can be unique in their viewpoint on tasks, options and projects, and look for a different way of doing things if there is an opportunity.

7. Service/ Dedication to a Cause - Those having this career anchor are driven by the idea of giving back. They typical are service-oriented and want to help others in a variety of ways – from health to safety to education. Money typically is not a primary motivator for this group, and appreciation is a major driver for their satisfaction.

8. Pure Challenge - Individuals that have Pure Challenge want to climb a mountain because it is there. The more impossible the mission, the more they want to attempt it. They are excited by a problem the do not know the answer or beating the odds.

Politics at work

"Politics is when people choose their words and actions based on how they want others to react rather than based on what they really think." — Patrick Lencioni, <u>The Five Dysfunctions of a Team: A Leadership Fable</u>

Politics at work is about expectation, understanding, choice, and setting. It's not about doing someone else' bidding as much is it about helping others get to the same result you have – by adapting to their personality.

For example – If you know others – their personality, attitudes, and mindsets- you know what to expect. If you understand them – then you know their "why" – their motivation.

How to use it as a leader: Translate <u>what</u> you say. You don't have to lie or say something untruthful – just use their style. Work with someone who's direct? Give it to them straight. Work with someone who may cry? Tell them gently (but firmly – to make sure the message gets across)

Learning & Managing personalities

There are many ways to learn the personalities, strengths, and motivation of your team. You could have one-one-one meetings – a great way to get to know them on an individual level. However, you may not have the time to dedicate in the short term, so you may find an opportunity to use an assessment.

There are a number of assessments to help with learning personality and what motivates individuals. The challenge is picking the one that you want. That is easier said than done. For assessments such as the Myers-Briggs Type Indicator (MBTI) or Gallup's Clifton Strengths, the output is only as good as the input—and someone in your organization must determine if the output is what is required to improve the talent on your team.

Why is motivation important?

Adapted from: *Go Beyond the Job Description*

There are two kinds of motivation—intrinsic and extrinsic. *Intrinsic motivation* is the kind that comes—yes, you guessed it—internally. You do it because you want to and because it makes you feel good. After all, it's a challenge. You don't necessarily need someone to pat you on the back and say you've done a good job. Both intrinsic and extrinsic motivation can inspire you at the same time. Extrinsic motivation gives you energy—the drive to do more—based on your external environment. For example, your boss recognizes you in front of the entire department for a job well done on a project. You get a raise or a promotion. Someone or something has given you recognition—and that is a motivation for you.

Now, take a look at your answers to the question of what motivates you. How quickly were you able to answer that question? Let's say your boss walks in the door right now and says to you, "You're going to a new job." This job will have *none* of the work motivation items on your list. What's more, you may lose other factors that motivate you, such as more time with your family.

Research has proven that giving individuals more of what motivates them increases their engagement—by as much as 25% (Prisant-Lesko, 2015). Here's a basic fact. People do what they do based on motivation. Good or bad, motivation drives what we do every day. Find out what motivates your team, and you'll increase their engagement.

Acknowledgements

This book came at a time where much was unknown. Unknown steps, actions, strategies, and challenges became the name of the game and what was once considered outlandish soon became a "New Normal".

I would like to thank several people for their contribution for their help during this time. From editing and giving feedback to giving pushback (even more pushback!), they took time out of their own "New Normal" to help make this book a reality. Special thanks to Maria Ortega, Dorothy Chaney, Monica Young, Zoë Mercurio, Tomm Larson, and Shiva Venkatraman. Thank you for suggestions from Estibali Carrera, Anthony Braekevelt, Kristen Maple and Stephen Lumayag.

Thank you to Jonathan and Sydney who never let me forget why I am doing what I do… and always, always… take time to watch Stretch and the chickadees.

And finally, thank you to my family for putting up with me (and my crazy ideas) … both now and for years. Your encouragement continues to fuel that fire.

And… when you're given a bag of lemons…. Make lemonade. Or… some variation of it.

References

#1 - Strategy & Pivot Tactics

Comeback Tactics

Becdach, C., Brown, B., Halbardier, F., Henstorf, B. & Murphy, R. (2020). *Rapidly forecasting demand and adapting commercial plans in a pandemic.* McKinsey Publishing. Retrieved from: https://www.mckinsey.com/industries/consumer-packaged-goods/our-insights/rapidly-forecasting-demand-and-adapting-commercial-plans-in-a-pandemic?

Rumelt, R. (2020). *Managing after the structural break.* McKinsey Publishing. Retrieved from- https://www.mckinsey.com/business-functions/strategy-and-corporate-finance/our-insights/strategy-in-a-structural-break?

Sneader, K. & Sternfels, B. (2020). *From Surviving to Thriving: Reimaging the post-COVID 19 return* McKinsey Publishing. Retrieved from: https://www.mckinsey.com/featured-insights/future-of-work/from-surviving-to-thriving-reimagining-the-post-covid-19-return?

Agile/ Digital Recovery / Other Strategy

Comella-Dorda, S., Garg, L., Thareja, S., & Vasquez-McCall, B. (2020). *Revisiting Agile teams after an abrupt shift to remote.* McKinsey Publishing. Retrieved from: Agile approaches to shifting back to work: https://www.mckinsey.com/business-functions/organization/our-insights/revisiting-agile-teams-after-an-abrupt-shift-to-remote?

Fitzpatrick, M., Gill, I., Libarikian, A., Smaje, K., & Zemmel, R., (2020). *The digital-led recovery from COVID-19: Five questions for CEO's.* McKinsey Publishing. Retrieved from:

https://www.mckinsey.com/business-functions/mckinsey-digital/our-insights/the-digital-led-recovery-from-covid-19-five-questions-for-ceos?

Kleiner, A., Thomson, J., Schwartz, J. (2019). *The wise advocate: The inner voice of strategic leadership.* Columbia Business School, New York, NY.

#2 - People

Berinato, S. (2020). *That discomfort you're feeling is grief.* Harvard Business Review. March 2020
Retrieved from https://hbr.org/2020/03/that-discomfort-youre-feeling-is-grief

McFeely, S. &Wigert,B., (2019). *This fixable problem costs U.S. Businesses $1 Trillion.* Gallup Inc. Retrieved from:
https://www.gallup.com/workplace/247391/fixable-problem-costs-businesses-trillion.aspx

#3 & #4 - Analysis & Action Plan

Stack, J. & Burlington, Bo. (2013). *Great Game of Business.* Crown Publishing Group. New York, NY.

Schrage, M. (2010). *Know your intuition.* Harvard Business Review. May 2010. Retrieved from https://hbr.org/2010/05/your-gut-is-overrated-really.html

Pedersen, C. L. & Ritter, T. (2020). *Preparing your business for a post-pandemic world..* Harvard Business Review. April 2020. Retrieved from https://hbr.org/2020/04/preparing-your-business-for-a-post-pandemic-world?

Motivation/ Career-related topics

Bennis, W. & Thomas, R.J. (2002). *Crucibles of Leadership*. Harvard Business Review. September 2002. Retrieved from https://hbr.org/2002/09/crucibles-of-leadership

Lencioni, P. (2002). *The five dysfunctions of a team: A Leadership fable*. Jossey-Bass Publishing. San Francisco, CA.

Prisant Lesko, A. (2019). *Go Beyond the Job Description*. SHRM Publication. Alexandria, VA.

Schein, E. H., & Van Maanen, J. (2013). *Career Anchors: The Changing Nature of Work and Careers*. Fourth Edition. Wiley Publishing, San Francisco, CA.

Tigar, L. (2019). *Eight signs you should quit your job.* January 2019. Retrieved from https://www.fastcompany.com/90288009/8-signs-you-should-quit-your-job

Trunk, P. (2009). *Don't try to dodge the recession with grad school.* Retrieved from https://blog.penelopetrunk.com/2009/02/03/dont-try-to-dodge-the-recession-with-grad-school/

Zimmerman, Ellen. (2009). *A recession may be a good time to go back to school.* January 2009. Retrieved from https://www.nytimes.com/2009/01/04/jobs/04career.html

Communication & Accountability

Prisant Lesko, A. (2015). *New Manager Influences: Probing the effects of career motivation on work engagement*. Sullivan University, Louisville, KY.